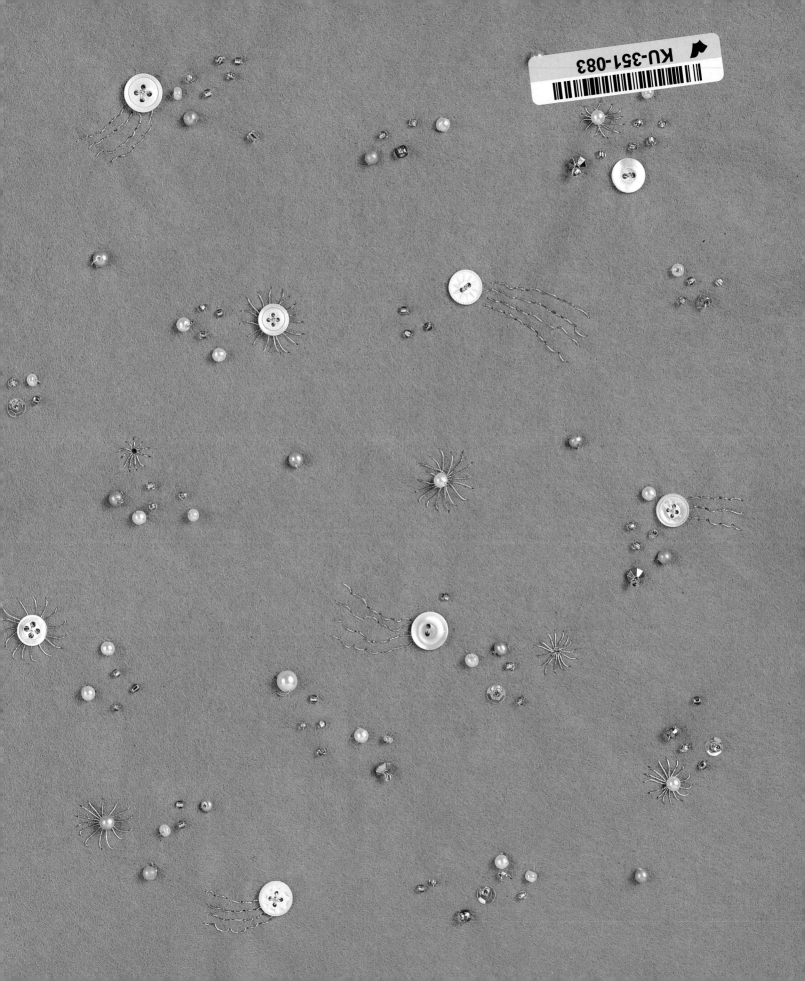

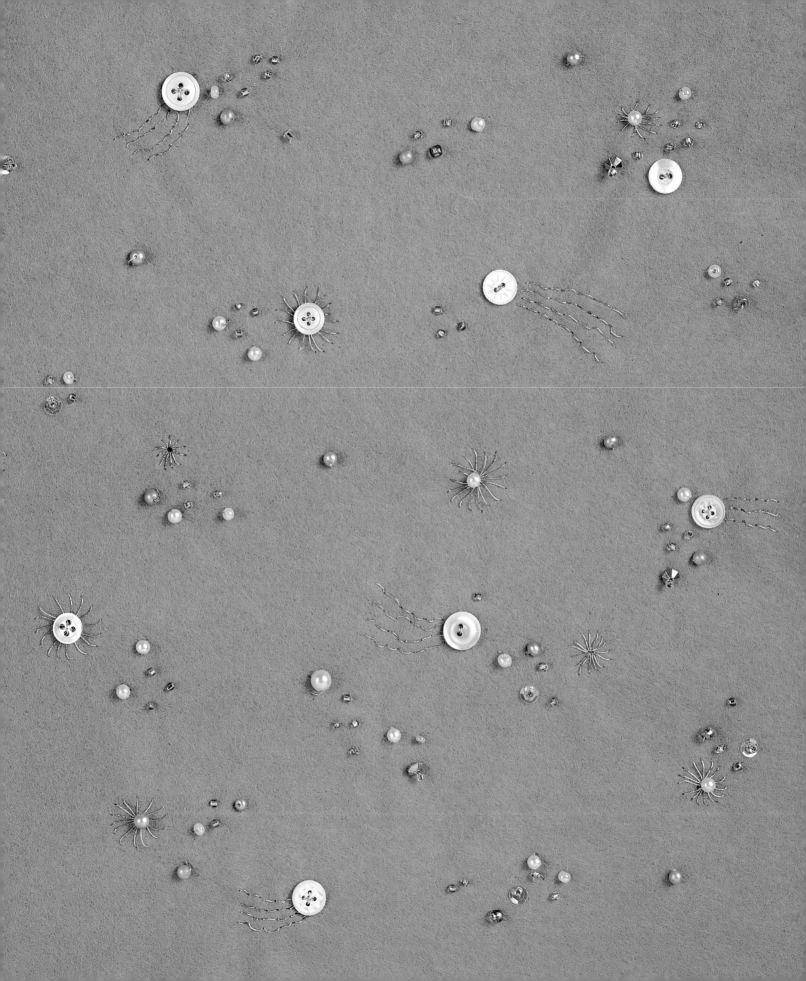

Mrs Moon
Sitting up in the sky;
Little old lady
Rock-a-bye.
With a ball of fading light
And silvery needles
Knitting the night.

Sweet dreams
for children
everywhere – C. B.

Barefoot Books, 124 Walcot Street, Bath, BA1 5BG

Illustrations copyright © 2003 by Clare Beaton
The moral right of Clare Beaton to be identified as the illustrator of this
work has been asserted

First published in Great Britain in 2003 by Barefoot Books, Ltd

This book was typeset in Celestia Antiqua 18 on 24 point. The illustrations were prepared
in antique fabrics and felt with braid, buttons, beads and assorted bric-a-brac. Graphic design
by Judy Linard, London. Colour transparencies by Jonathan Fisher Photography, Bath.
Colour separation by Grafiscan, Verona. Printed and bound in Singapore by Tien Wah Press.
This book has been printed on 100% acid-free paper.

ISBN 1-84148-062-2

British Library Cataloguing-in-Publication Data:
A catalogue record for this book is available from the British Library

1 3 5 7 9 8 6 4 2

MRS. MOON
Lullabies for Bedtime

Clare Beaton

Barefoot Books
Celebrating Art and Story

CONTENTS

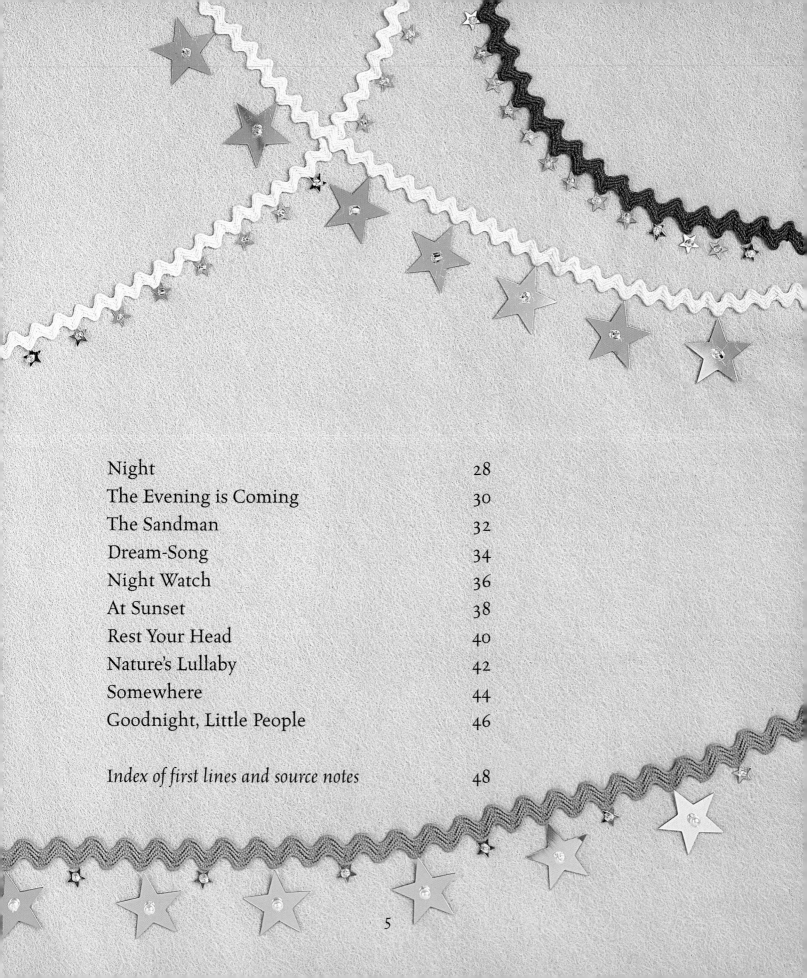

ROCK-A-BYE, BABY

Rock-a-bye, baby, on the tree top,
When the wind blows the cradle will rock.
When the bough breaks, the cradle will fall,
And down will come baby, cradle and all.

CUSHLAMOCHREE

Cushlamochree, O Cushlamochree,
Shall you dance for the stars?
Shall you play with the sea?
Shall you swim like the whale?
Shall you follow the sun?
O Cushlamochree, has your dreaming begun?

Cariad Bach, O Cariad Bach,
Shall you sing to the moon?
Shall you shout for the dark?
Shall you whisper with bears?
Shall you waken the night?
O Cariad Bach, soft dreams and sleep tight.

('Cushlamochree' is Gaelic for 'darling'; 'Cariad Bach' is
Gaelic for 'Little Darling')

9

ALL THE PRETTY LITTLE HORSES

Hush-you-bye, don't you cry,
Go to sleepy, little baby.
When you wake, you shall have
All the pretty little horses –
Blacks and bays, dapples and greys,
Coach and six-a-little horses.

NEIGH

NEIGH

TRIT TROT   CLIP CLOP   CLIP CLOP

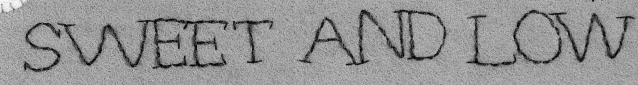

SWEET AND LOW

Sweet and low, sweet and low,
Wind of the western sea,
Low, low, breathe and blow,
Wind of the western sea!
Over the rolling waters go,
Come from the dying moon, and blow,
Blow him again to me;
While my little one, while my pretty one, sleeps.

HUSH, LITTLE BABY

Hush, little baby, don't say a word,
Papa's going to buy you a mocking bird.

And if that mocking bird don't sing,
Papa's going to buy you a diamond ring.

And if that diamond ring turns to brass,
Papa's going to buy you a looking-glass.

And if that looking-glass gets broke,
Papa's going to buy you a billy-goat.

And if that billy-goat don't pull,
Papa's going to buy you a cart and bull.

WOOF!

And if that cart and bull turn over,
Papa's going to buy you a dog named Rover.

And if that dog named Rover won't bark,
Papa's going to buy you a horse and cart.

And if that horse and cart fall down,
You'll still be the cutest little baby in town.

15

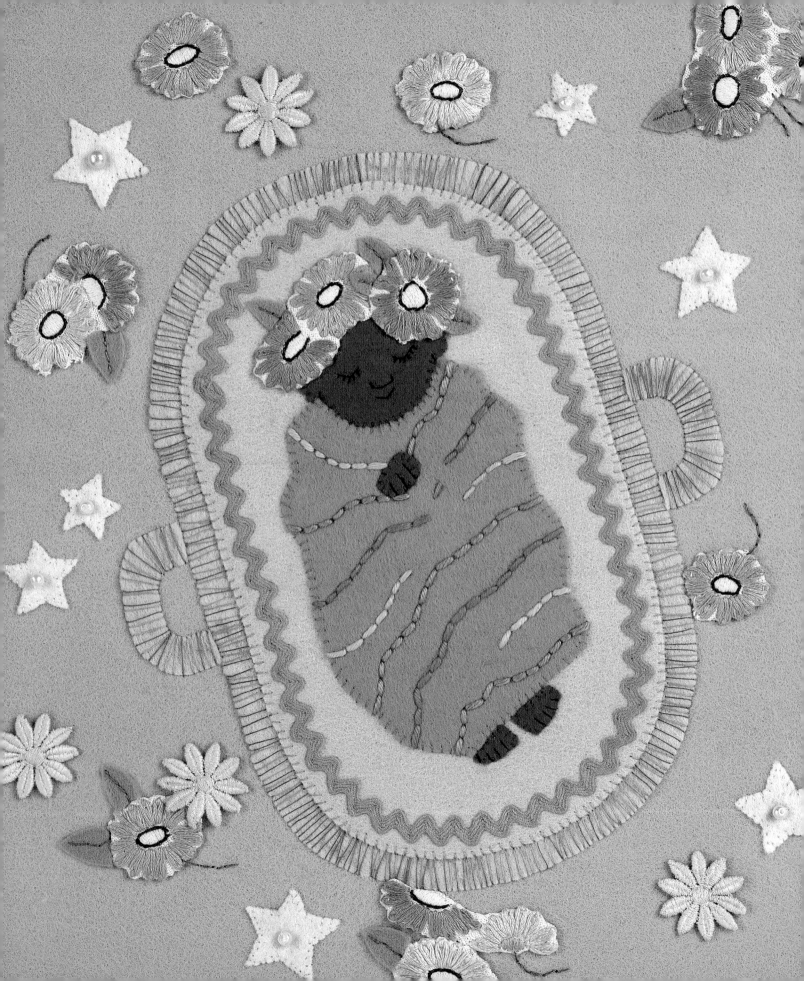

BRAHMS' LULLABY

Lullaby and goodnight,
In the sky stars are bright.
Round your head flowers gay
Scent your slumbers till day.
Close your eyes now and rest,
May these hours be blest.
Go to sleep now and rest,
May these hours be blest.

ONLY THE MOON HAS SECRETS

Only the moon has secrets,
The moon in her silvery home,
And in this hour of the evening
She'll share them with you alone.

You can trust the moon to hold you,
Keep you from fear or from harm,
Go with the moon on her journey,
Feel yourself safe in her arms.

Keep what you see on the journey,
Keep what you see as your own,
After the bright silver journey,
I'll whisper you all the way home.

MIDNIGHT SONG

If you may if you might
Stay up deep into the night
Sending all your dreams and wishes
Up to the Moon
Like silver fishes
Travelling on in waves of prayer
Like ripples through a mermaid's hair
And wait till they come curling back
And then fall quietly on your lap
Leaving answers gifts and rainbows
So gentle that they only glow
In your eyes when you awake
A reflection of the world you make

DEEP IN THE BUSH

Deep in the bush
There's a brown mother mouse,
She's singing a song
In her cosy bush house.
'Goodnight my mousies,
Sweet dreams, sleep tight.
I kiss your whiskers
And whisper
Good night!'

THE BOATIE BABY'S LULLABY

Little waves are dancing,
They're skipping on the shore.
Such a gentle curling
You'll always hear, and more.

Hush while the waves are busy,
Let your sea dreams fly.
Hear the sparkles in the water –
Our boaties' lullaby.

Let the deep sea rock you,
While the crickle-crackle sings,
Twinkle for your sweet sea dreams
Of fish and sandy things.

Hush while the waves are busy,
Let your sea dreams fly.
Hear the sparkles in the water –
Our boaties' lullaby.

SEAL LULLABY

Oh! hush thee, my baby, the night is behind us,
And black are the waters that sparkled so green.
The moon, o'er the combers, looks downwards to find us
At rest in the hollows that rustle between.

Where billow meets billow, there soft be thy pillow;
Ah, weary wee flipperling, curl at thy ease!
The storm shall not wake thee, nor shark overtake thee,
Asleep in the arms of the slow-swinging seas.

NIGHT

The sun descending in the west,
The evening star does shine;
The birds are silent in their nests,
And I must seek for mine.
The moon like a flower,
In heaven's high bower,
With silent delight
Sits and smiles on the night.

THE EVENING IS COMING

The evening is coming, the sun sinks to rest,
The birds are all flying straight home to their nests.
'Caw, caw,' says the crow as he flies overhead.
It's time little children were going to bed.

Here comes the pony, his work is all done,
Down through the meadow he takes a good run.
Up go his heels, and down goes his head.
It's time little children were going to bed.

THE SANDMAN

The flowers are sleeping
Beneath the moon's soft light,
With heads close together
They dream through the night.
And leafy trees rock to and fro
And whisper low –
Sleep, sleep, lullaby,
O sleep, my darling child.

Now birds that sang sweetly,
To greet the morning sun,
In little nests are sleeping
Now twilight has begun.
The cricket chirps its sleepy song,
Its dreamy song –
Sleep, sleep, lullaby,
O sleep, my darling child.

The Sandman comes on tiptoe
And through the window peeps,
To see if little children
Are in their beds asleep.
And when a little child he finds
Casts sand in his eyes –
Sleep, sleep, lullaby,
O sleep, my darling child.

DREAM-SONG

Sunlight, moonlight,
Twilight, starlight –
Gloaming at the close of day,
And an owl calling,
Cool dews falling
In a wood of oak and may.

Lantern-light, taper-light,
Torchlight, no-light;
Darkness at the shut of day,
And lions roaring,
Their wrath pouring
In wild waste places far away.

Elf-light, bat-light;
Touchwood-light and toad-light,
And the sea a shimmering gloom of grey,
And a small face smiling
In a dream's beguiling
In a world of wonders far away.

NIGHT WATCH

The cradle is warm
And there shall you sleep
Safe and warm, little baby.
Angels shall come
And stand closely to keep
Watch over you, little baby.
Bye-bye now, go to sleep,
So sweetly to sleep, little baby.

AT SUNSET

In the evening
The sun goes down,
And the lamps are lit
In the little town.

38

The bats fly low
Round the grey church dome,
The thrush and the blackbird
Are safely home –

Are safely home
In their quiet nest –
The thrush and the blackbird
Are both at rest!

REST YOUR HEAD

Rest your head upon my shoulder,
Baby, little baby.

Sleepy head, your day is over,
Baby, little baby.

Close your eyes while I sing a lullaby,
Baby, baby of mine,
Baby, baby of mine.

Let me rock you in my arms,
Baby, little baby.

I will keep you safe and warm,
Baby, little baby.

Have the sweetest dreams, you mean everything to me,
Baby, baby of mine,
Baby, baby of mine.

NATURE'S LULLABY

Warm in their woolly folds,
Lambkins are resting;
Soft in their swaying beds,
Birdies are nesting;
All through the night,
In your cradle lie dreaming,
'Til the bright sun
Through the window comes streaming.

Hush-a-bye, baby,
The night winds are sighing;
Go to sleep, baby,
The crickets are crying;
Sleep 'til the dew
On the green grass is winking,
Sleep 'til the morning sun
Wakens you blinking.

Off in the distance
A hoot owl is calling;
Into sweet dreams
Little babes should be falling;
Hush-a-bye, baby,
It's time you were sleeping,
'Til rays of sunlight
At morning come creeping.

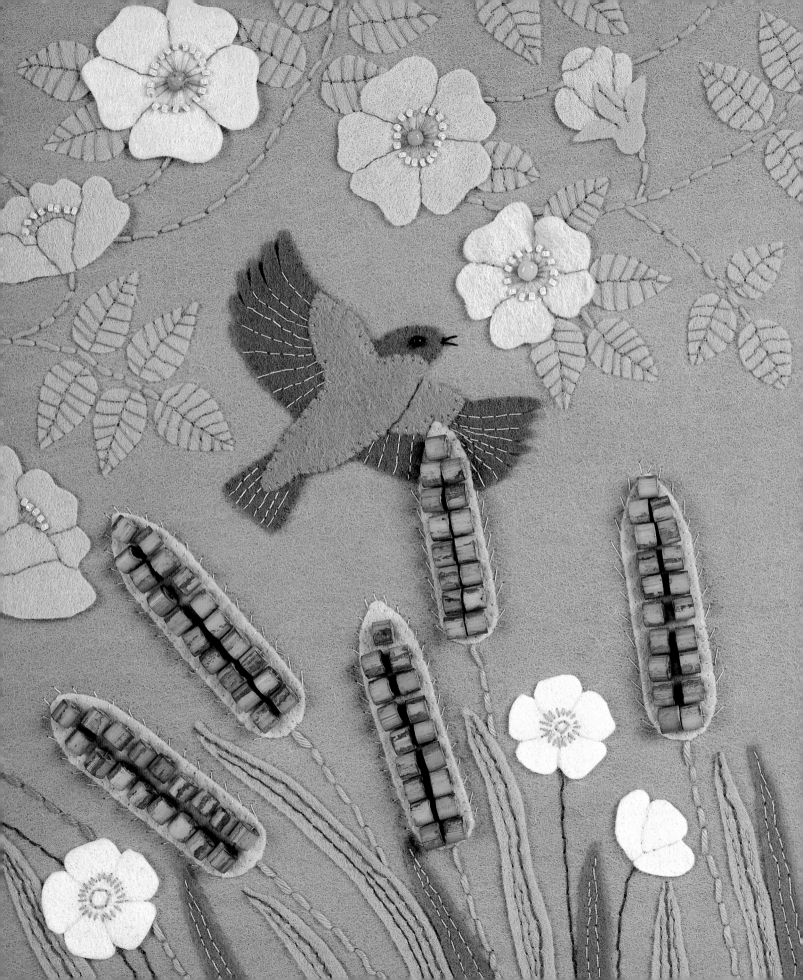

SOMEWHERE

Whenever a little child is born,
All night a soft wind rocks the corn;
One more buttercup wakes to the morn,
Somewhere, somewhere.

And one more rosebud will soon unfold,
And one more birdsong the air will hold,
One more cricket whose tale will be told,
Somewhere, somewhere.

Whenever a little child is born,
All night a gentle breeze rocks the corn;
One more buttercup blooms in the morn,
Somewhere, somewhere.

GOODNIGHT, LITTLE PEOPLE

The evening is coming,
The sun sinks to rest;
The rooks are all flying
Straight home to the nest;
'Caw,' says the rook
As he flies overhead,
'It's time little people
Were going to bed.'

The butterfly, drowsy,
Has folded its wing;
The bees are returning,
No more the birds sing;
Their labour is over,
Their nestlings are fed,
'It's time little people
Were going to bed.'

The flowers are closing,
The daisy's asleep,
The primrose is buried
In slumber so deep.
And closed for the night
Are the roses so red,
'It's time little people
Were going to bed.'

Goodnight, little people,
Goodnight and goodnight;
Sweet dreams to your eyelids
Till dawning of light.
The evening has come,
There's no more to be said,
'It's time little people
Were going to bed.'

INDEX OF FIRST LINES

Acknowledgements and Sources

'At Sunset' written by Ivy O. Eastwick.

'The Boatie Baby's Lullaby' copyright © Trish Gribben, 'Deep in the Bush' copyright © Michelanne Forster and 'Only the Moon Has Secrets' copyright © John Marsden, all from *A Book of Pacific Lullabies*, edited by Tessa Duder and illustrated by Anton Petrov, HarperCollinsPublishers (New Zealand) Limited.

'Dream Song' written by Walter de la Mare.

'Midnight Song' copyright © Louise Amelia, Visionary Arts 2000.

'Nature's Lullaby' Scottish folk-song.

'Night' written by William Blake.

'Rest Your Head', Atkins/Bradley/Nabb/Wilson, copyright © Fastforward Music Ltd.

'Seal Lullaby' written by Rudyard Kipling.

'Somewhere' written by Agnes Carter.

'Sweet and Low' written by Alfred, Lord Tennyson, composed by Sir Joseph Barnby, from *The Parlour Song Book* (1972).

The publishers have made every effort to contact holders of copyright material. If you have not received our correspondence, please contact us for inclusion in future editions.

Barefoot Books
Celebrating Art and Story

At Barefoot Books, we celebrate art and story with books that open the hearts and minds of children from all walks of life, inspiring them to read deeper, search further, and explore their own creative gifts. Taking our inspiration from many different cultures, we focus on themes that encourage independence of spirit, enthusiasm for learning, and acceptance of other traditions. Thoughtfully prepared by writers, artists and storytellers from all over the world, our products combine the best of the present with the best of the past to educate our children as the caretakers of tomorrow.

www.barefootbooks.com

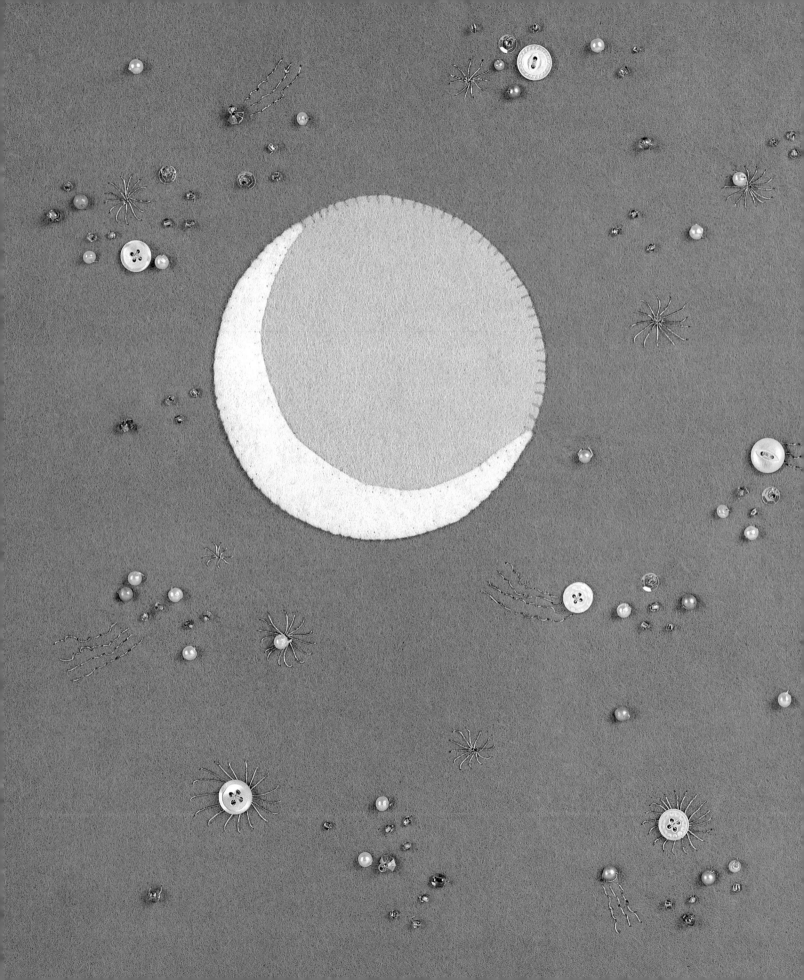